Facing the Future
CHOOSING HEALTH

Facing the Future
CHOOSING HEALTH

Alan Collinson

STECK-VAUGHN
LIBRARY
A Division of Steck-Vaughn Company

Austin, Texas

Published 1991 by Steck-Vaughn Co., Austin, Texas

Library of Congress Cataloging-in-Publication Data

Collinson, Alan.
      Choosing health / by Alan Collinson.
          p. cm. – (Facing the future)
      Includes index.
      Summary: Discusses many aspects of health, including diet, exercise, genetic factors, the body's defense system, mental attitude, and medicine.
      ISBN 0-8114-2801-X
      1. Health—Juvenile literature.   2. Medical innovations—Juvenile literature.   3. Environmental health—Juvenile literature.
      [1. Health.]   I. Title.   II. Series.
      RA776.5.065   1991
      613—dc20   90-25849
                                                              CIP
                                                               AC

Typeset by David Seham Associates, Metuchen, NJ
Printed in Hong Kong.
Bound in the United States
1 2 3 4 5 6 7 8 9 0 HK 95 94 93 92 91

Acknowledgments

Maps and diagrams – Jillian Luff of Bitmap Graphics
Illustrations – Outline Illustration, Derby – Andrew Calvert, Andrew Cook, Andrew Staples
Design – Neil Sayer
Editor – Su Swallow

For permission to reproduce copyright material the author and publishers gratefully acknowledge the following:

Cover photograph *A medical technician observes a laser treatment at the Bethesda Naval hospital in Maryland.–© Bruce Hoertel/Gamma Liaison.*

Title page *–Exercise is a principal means of maintaining good health throughout a lifetime. –Zefa*

Page 5 – Nancy Durrell McKenna, Hutchison Library; page 6 – (top) Trygve Bølstad, Panos Pictures – (bottom) James Green, Robert Harding Picture Library; page 8 – John Young, Intermediate Technology; page 9 – Mark Boulton, Bruce Coleman Limited; page 10 – Linda Pitkin, Planet Earth Pictures; page 11 – (top) Dept of Clinical Cytogenetics, Addenbrookes Hospital, Cambridge, Science Photo Library – (main picture) Philippe Plailly; Science Photo Library – (bottom) Div. of Computer Research and Technology, National Institute of Health, Science Photo Library; page 12 – Philippe Plailly, Science Photo Library; page 13 – Martin Birley, Tropix; page 14 – J.G. Fuller, Hutchison Library; page 16 – (left) Mary Jory, Tropix – (right) Barbara Klass, Panos Pictures; page 17 – Tim Shepherd, Oxford Scientific Films; page 18 – Zefa; page 19 – David Maitland, Planet Earth Pictures; page 20 – (left) Heather Angel – (inset) Christina Dodwell, Hutchison Library – (right) Andrew Mounter, Planet Earth Pictures; page 21 – (main picture) Adrian Evans, Panos Pictures; page 22 – (left) Armin Svoboda, Planet Earth Pictures – (right) Dr T. Blundell, Dept. of Crystallography, Birbeck College, Science Photo Library; page 23 – (left) M.J. Flügel, Bruce Coleman Limited – (right) Prato, Bruce Coleman Limited; page 24 – Zefa; page 25 – (top left) Alexander Tsiaras, Science Photo Library – (bottom left) H. Sochurek, Zefa – (right) Robert Goldstein, Science Photo Library; page 26 – Sarah Errington, Hutchison Library; page 27 – Dr Robin Williams, Science Photo Library; page 28 – Associated Press, Topham; page 29 – (main picture) Larry Mulvehill, Science Photo Library – (inset) Alexander Tsiaras, Science Photo Library; page 30 – (main picture) Martin Bond, Science Photo Library – (inset) Zefa; page 31 – Michael Macintyre, Hutchison Library; page 32 – (left) German Castro, Panos Pictures – (right) V.J. Birley, Tropix; page 33 – Liba Taylor, Hutchison Library; page 34 – Peter Menzel, Science Photo Library; page 35 – Martin Dohrn, Science Photo Library; page 37 – (top left) James Green, Robert Harding Picture Library – (bottom left) The Hulton Picture Company – (right) Stuart Wylie; page 39 – The Horniman Museum, London; page 40 – (left) Damien Lovegrove, Science Photo Library – (bottom left) Paul Biddle and Tim Maylon, Science Photo Library – (right) Paul Biddle and Tim Maylon, Science Photo Library – (bottom right) Andrew McClenaghan, Science Photo Library; page 41 – Zefa; page 42 – M.Timothy O'Keefe, Bruce Coleman Limited; page 43 – Zefa.

Contents

Introduction 4

Increasing Life's Chances 6
Vital statistics   Polluted water   Health and wealth

Quest for a Cure 10
Reading the instructions for life   Changes for the better?

The Body's Own Defenses 14
The white knights   Vaccination: a shield against disease
Shielding the world   Developing new defenses

Magic Bullets 18
Counting the cost   Drugs from plants
Saving trees, saving life   Chemistry by computer
More than a Sweetener

Technology for Tomorrow 24
Seeing more clearly   Barefoot doctors
Computer-aided design   Consulting the computer
The gentle art of surgery

Hazards on the Road to Health 30
Danger at work   Taking risks   A messy world   Good food?
Cleaning up the mess   *Return of a Killer*

Prescription for Health 36
You are what you eat   Too much of a good thing
Too little of a good thing   Mind over matter   *Alternative Medicine*
Evolution, exercise, and health   Exploring inner space

A Long Life and a Healthy One 42
The four stages of life   Vitamins for vitality   Active aging
A gift of extra time

Glossary 44

Further Reading 44

Index 45

Introduction

By the time you have finished reading this introduction at least 300 more people will have been added to the world's population. Most of these people will have been born in poor countries, and many will die before the age of five. Most of the people born in the rich countries can look forward to a long healthy life. At present the world is divided into rich countries with mostly healthy people and poor countries with widespread ill health. The burden of ill health on the poor countries often means that they find it difficult to develop their farming, industry, and education and cannot create the wealth to improve the lives of their people. For most people in these countries, living is a matter of survival from day to day.

In spite of all the infant deaths in poor countries, so many babies are born that the population of those countries—and therefore of the world—is rising rapidly. (At present it is over 5 billion. By the year 2020 it will be over 7 billion.) The United Nations has launched a campaign to try to ensure that every member of the world's rising population will have a healthy life. The United Nations has set a target date of 2000 for health for all. This target will only be achieved if the rich countries choose to help the poor countries. This is one of the most important choices for health in the future. If money and other resources are not provided, the prospects for world health are not good.

Around the world efforts to improve health are being made by many doctors, nurses, scientists, and ordinary people. But it is a race against time. As the population rises, these workers have to work even harder and the resources given by the rich countries have to be spread among even more people. At the same time the rich countries spend more and more on their own health. Many of the diseases that soak up resources in the rich countries could be prevented by more sensible choices in living—choices such as not smoking, drinking less alcohol, driving more slowly and carefully, eating more sensibly, and getting more exercise. The choice of health for all is not just something to be left to governments. It is a choice we can all make. If we choose sensibly in

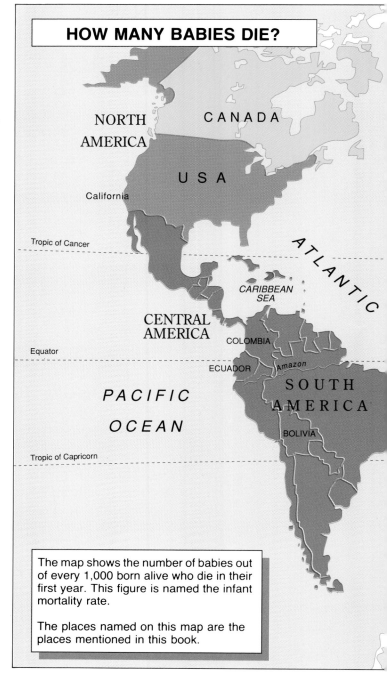

HOW MANY BABIES DIE?

The map shows the number of babies out of every 1,000 born alive who die in their first year. This figure is named the infant mortality rate.

The places named on this map are the places mentioned in this book.

our own lives, we leave resources available for other people who really need them.

In this book you will read about many of the advances in medical and scientific knowledge. Then you can start thinking about the choices for yourself. Some choices are simple: the choice not to smoke, for instance. Other choices are much more difficult and have never before been faced. They even include the choice of what sort of people we want to create in the future. This is not fantasy—scientists are already discussing the possibilities. Scientific research moves so fast that to start thinking about such choices now is not too soon!

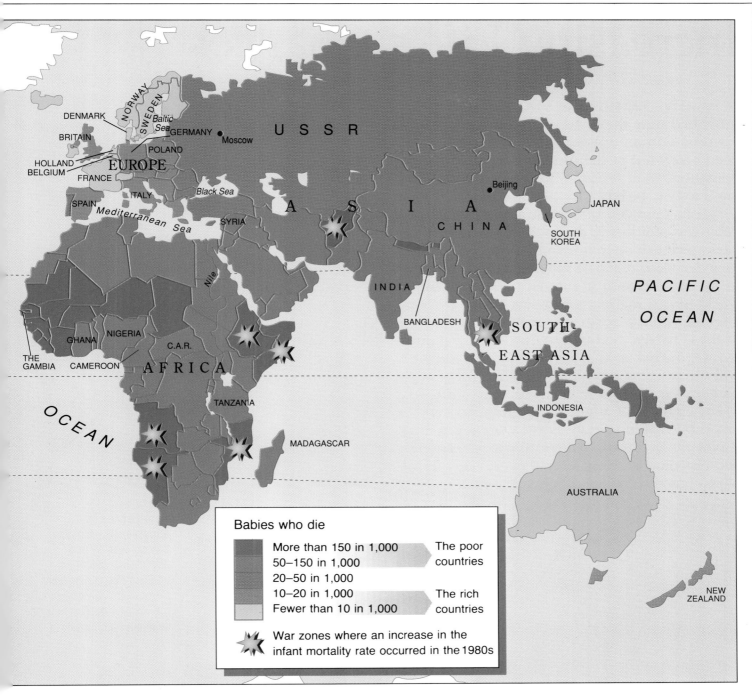

Babies who die

More than 150 in 1,000	The poor
50–150 in 1,000	countries
20–50 in 1,000	
10–20 in 1,000	The rich
Fewer than 10 in 1,000	countries

War zones where an increase in the infant mortality rate occurred in the 1980s

DENMARK
BRITAIN
HOLLAND
BELGIUM
FRANCE
EUROPE
SPAIN
ITALY
NORWAY
SWEDEN
Baltic Sea
GERMANY
POLAND
Moscow
USSR
Black Sea
Mediterranean Sea
SYRIA
ASIA
Beijing
CHINA
JAPAN
SOUTH KOREA
Nile
INDIA
PACIFIC OCEAN
THE GAMBIA
GHANA
NIGERIA
CAMEROON
C.A.R.
AFRICA
BANGLADESH
SOUTH EAST ASIA
OCEAN
TANZANIA
MADAGASCAR
INDONESIA
AUSTRALIA
NEW ZEALAND

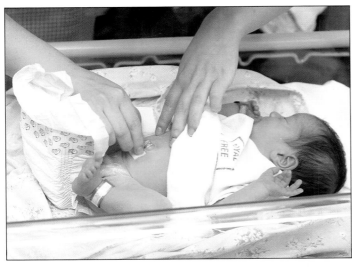

What will be the future for this newborn baby? Children born today face either a healthy future or an unhealthy one. The choice is ours.

Increasing Life's Chances

In January 1990 surgeons in California described how they had carried out an operation on an unborn baby. The baby had been taken out of the mother's womb for the operation, then returned to the womb until it was ready to be born. In the same month British surgeons operated on a baby's heart while the baby was still inside the mother's womb. To perform these operations, modern equipment, new drugs, and expert nursing care were used. In the same month in many countries of the world over a million babies were born without any help from machines or medical staff. Many of these babies died before they were a month old. Of the babies that survived, about one fifth will die before the age of five. In countries with plenty of medical care very few babies die.

The chances of a healthy life depend very much on where you are born. One important choice for the future is how to provide enough good medical services so that every baby in the world has the chance of a healthy life.

New arrivals in Bangladesh (above). Babies born in poor, developing countries are less likely to survive beyond the age of five than babies born in rich, developed countries.

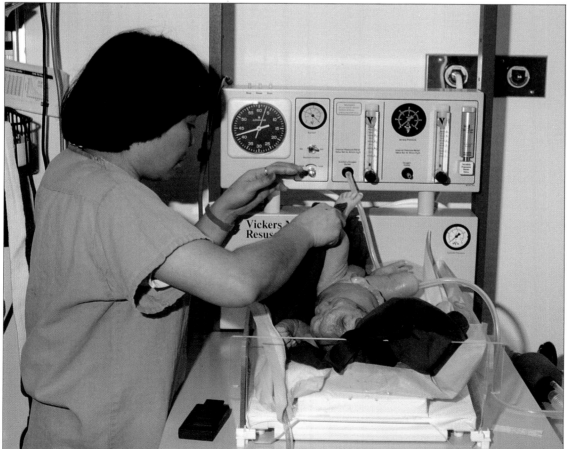

Hospital care. Developed countries can afford to provide modern machinery and skilled nursing care to give newborn babies a healthy start in life.

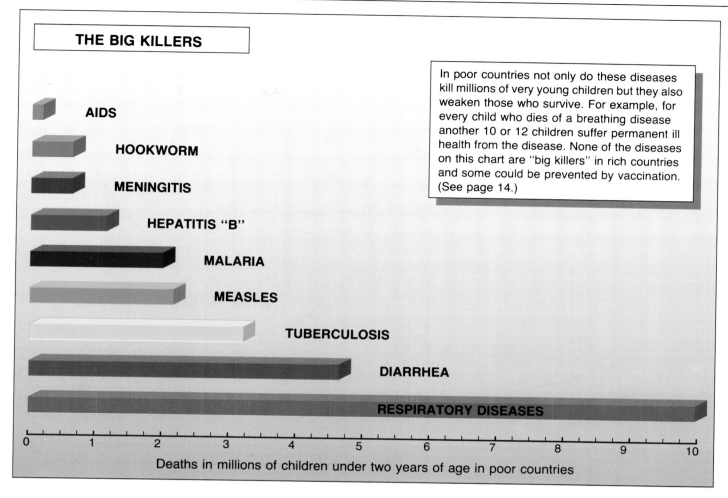

THE BIG KILLERS

- AIDS
- HOOKWORM
- MENINGITIS
- HEPATITIS "B"
- MALARIA
- MEASLES
- TUBERCULOSIS
- DIARRHEA
- RESPIRATORY DISEASES

In poor countries not only do these diseases kill millions of very young children but they also weaken those who survive. For example, for every child who dies of a breathing disease another 10 or 12 children suffer permanent ill health from the disease. None of the diseases on this chart are "big killers" in rich countries and some could be prevented by vaccination. (See page 14.)

Deaths in millions of children under two years of age in poor countries

0 1 2 3 4 5 6 7 8 9 10

Vital statistics

One way to find out if we are making the world a healthier place is to look at how many babies survive the first year of life. This is when children are most likely to catch diseases that could kill them. The figure that is used is the number of babies that die out of every 1,000 live babies born. This figure is called the **infant mortality rate.** In the United States the rate is about 10 babies in 1,000. In Japan it is four in 1,000. In poor countries the figure is usually much higher. For example, in the Central African Republic it is 134 in 1,000 and in India 98 in 1,000. You will see from the map on page 5 that the countries with high infant mortality rates are in South and Central America, Africa, and southern and eastern Asia. These are the poor (or developing) countries of the world. The countries with low infant mortality rates are rich, developed countries.

Polluted water

People in poor countries suffer from many diseases that could be prevented fairly easily. About 150 years ago many of these diseases, such as measles, tuberculosis, and diarrhea, were the big killers in rich countries as well. At that time, infant mortality figures were little better in rich countries than they are in poor countries now. However, from 1860—before scientists even knew what caused them—the diseases became less frequent in countries such as England, France, and Germany.

Doctors noticed that if people had clean water, proper bathrooms, and better food, they became healthier. In the 1850s there was a terrible outbreak of a deadly disease called cholera in London, England. One doctor, John Smith, suspected its source was a single public water pump in the northern part of the city. People lined up every day to fill their buckets at the pump. When he asked them to stop drinking the water they took no notice of him. The authorities ignored him as well. The cholera spread and more people died. Finally, Dr. Smith went to the pump one night and stole the handle so that the pump could not be used. Before the handle could be replaced the cholera began to subside. It was then discovered that the company that owned the pump was supplying it with river water polluted by sewage. A few years later, the queen of England's husband died from drinking water polluted by poor drains in the castle.

It was only after these experiences that the authorities began to accept the need for clean water. Soon the larger towns began to build good water and sewage systems. The outbreaks of cholera, measles, whooping cough, scarlet fever, diphtheria, and other deadly diseases fell, so many more children survived. At the same time, industry, trade, and agriculture began to improve. People ate better and were strong enough to fight off some diseases. The whole population began to live longer. This improvement in healthy conditions has continued to the present day.

We know that if the poor countries had the three essentials for health—clean water, good drains and sewage systems, and a good diet—their people's health would improve and many more of their children would survive as well. However, these essentials cost money. Where is the money to come from?

Health and wealth

In the 1960s and 1970s rich countries gave money to poor countries to improve their water, sewage, medical services, and agriculture. More children survived and people lived longer. However, in the 1980s this improvement began to slow down as spending on health care fell in many poor countries.

Why did poor countries cut back on health care? In order to pay back the large amounts of money they had borrowed, poor countries were forced to cut spending on things that did not make money. Spending on health, education, land improvement, and housing was cut.

The United Nations has recommended that rich countries give aid to poor countries to the amount of 0.7 percent of the wealth they produce each year. So far only Norway, Holland, Sweden, and Denmark contribute this much. The United States gives only 0.2 percent. Other rich countries such as Japan, Britain, Australia, New Zealand, and France give only a little more. Not all of the aid helps the local people, either. Some countries, such as Japan and Britain, give a lot of their aid for projects such as mining and logging in tropical forests. These activities can ruin the natural resources that poor countries will need for the future. The United Nations program "Health for all by 2000" can only be achieved if enough aid of the right kind is given to developing countries.

Keeping a check. These mothers in Gambia (above) have brought their babies to a clinic for a checkup. As more such clinics are set up in developing countries, more children will survive into adulthood.

Clean water? The greatest danger to health in poor countries is polluted water. The water in this river in Nigeria (left) is clean now. However, as the population rises, the water could become polluted unless efficient sewage systems are provided.

Fit for Thought?
● Find out from your parents, grandparents, and other relatives what kinds of diseases they suffered from as children. Ask them how they were treated. Are the diseases and treatments the same today?
● Ask your parents about the illnesses you have had since you were born. Multiply the average figure in a class by three to give you an idea of how many illnesses a child in a poor country will have had by the same age.

infanty mortality rate – the number of babies that die out of every 1,000 live babies born.

Quest for a Cure

One of the world's rarest animals lives in one small pool on the coast of a Pacific island. The animal is a certain type of coral, and it contains one of the most complex chemicals ever discovered. The chemical, palytoxin, is so complicated that it took scientists eight years to find out its structure and then make the same chemical in a laboratory. This work will help scientists to understand how chemicals in our bodies work.

There are many causes of illness. Sometimes toxins are taken into the body. We may eat spoiled food or drink polluted water. In addition, disease-causing **microbes,** or tiny organisms, may enter the body. Microbes, such as bacteria and viruses, cause a range of illnesses from polio and smallpox to chicken pox and measles. In other cases, the body begins to malfunction for unknown reasons. For example, tissues in joints may begin to break down, causing arthritis.

In the future, medical research will concentrate more and more on the chemistry of disease. This is why work on complex chemicals such as palytoxin is so important. If we can work out the techniques to copy even the most complicated chemical known, we can use these techniques to prevent, treat, and cure many illnesses.

Corals to the rescue? Many soft-bodied animals such as slugs, snails, and corals produce poisons that protect them from being eaten. Knowing how these chemicals work can be helpful in making new medicines for people.

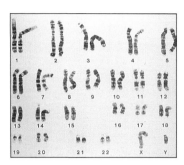

Looking for clues. Each human cell contains 23 pairs of chromosomes (above, magnified more than 1,000 times). Chromosomes are made up of a chemical called DNA. A model of DNA is shown below. A section of DNA that codes for one trait is called a gene. The computer printout (right) gives details of just 15 plant genes. A person may carry as many as half a million genes!

Reading the instructions for life

Chemicals in our bodies are produced by the cells, or the living units, of our bodies. Each cell contains a set of chemical instructions that directs it. Each instruction is called a **gene.** The genes are linked together in long chains called chromosomes. Scientists are now learning to decode genes. Understanding these genetic instructions will lead to a better understanding of the body and of the causes of disease and the way the body defends itself. Many diseases might be prevented or cured.

The total of all the genes in any plant or animal is called its **genome.** In 1989 a huge worldwide project was launched to study all the genes of the human genome. As the genome contains millions of bits of information (see photograph on page 11) the project will probably go on well into the next century. Some genes have already been identified. For instance, in 1989 the single gene for the disease called cystic fibrosis was identified. Children who are born with this disease produce too much mucus in their lungs. The condition is very difficult to treat and the children usually die young. Now that we know where the gene for the disease is located on the chromosome, we can begin to work out how to correct it. First, though, we must find out who carries the gene. We know that about one person in 20 has a copy of the gene. You may carry it yourself. Only when both parents carry the gene can the disease be passed on to their child. By screening (testing) couples, doctors can warn them of any risks before they have children.

There are many diseases that can be inherited from one's parents in the same way as cystic fibrosis. Unfortunately, many of these diseases involve more than one gene. However, finding out where the genes are in the genome, and what they do chemically, will be a great step forward. Scientists may then be able to make drugs that cure the illness or even "switch off" the instructions in the genes before they can do any damage.

Changes for the better?

In 1990 scientists put human genes into a new breed of mice so that the animals could be used to test drugs against AIDS. Moving genes from one animal or plant to another is called **genetic engineering.** It has been used for a number of years in the plant and animal breeding industries. For example, in the United States there is now a new breed of pigs that are not really pigs. They have been produced by combining pig genes with those of cattle. The resulting animals are larger and leaner than traditional pigs. Plant breeders are putting genes from plants such as peas into wheat, other grain crops, and soybeans. Peas can make their own fertilizer from nitrogen in the air; the hope is that these other crops will eventually be able to do the same. By using this kind of genetic engineering, scientists hope that some plants may be given the genetic instructions to enable them to make drugs. The soybean, for example, may be genetically engineered to produce large quantities of **antibodies** to kill cold and flu viruses. (See page 14.)

Farming for medicine (above right). This soybean crop in Tanzania is being grown for food. In the future a new form of soybean may be grown that will produce antibodies for many kinds of diseases.

Genetic engineering will allow scientists to alter plants so that they produce chemicals for use in drugs.

It is easy to see the possible benefits of genetic engineering. However, such knowledge also presents us with very dangerous choices. At present, genetic engineering consists of splitting chromosomes and inserting other genes. The long-term aim is to alter the genes themselves. Some people are worried about what could happen when scientists are able to do this.

You probably know people who are particularly good at math or music or sports, or who learn things easily. We are all good at doing certain things. Our talents are partly a result of our genes. If we knew how to change these genes we could "design" people with particular talents. Would this be a good thing? This could be the most important choice that human beings will ever have to face. It goes well beyond simply wanting to make people healthier. The science of genetics is developing so fast that this choice may not be far away.

Fit for Thought?
● What do you think about the idea of "designing" people? Who do you think should make such designs?

microbes – microscopic organisms: bacteria, viruses, and fungi (see glossary on page 44).
gene – the instructions for a single characteristic or trait of an animal or plant.
genome – all the genes of a particular kind of plant or animal (a species) that can be inherited.
genetic engineering – moving genes around either within an animal or plant or from one kind of animal or plant to another.
antibodies – chemicals produced in the human body that fight disease.

The Body's Own Defenses

The world around us is full of chemical dangers. Even as we breathe we are taking in pollen, dust, **bacteria, viruses,** and so on. Any of these could cause chemical damage to the body and make us ill. The reason they do not usually do so is because our bodies have their own built-in defenses.

The white knights

As blood circulates through our bodies it carries with it two main kinds of cells: red cells, which carry oxygen and white cells—sometimes called the white knights—which do a number of jobs in the body. They clear away dead cells and any loose fragments of material. But one of their most important jobs is to defend the body against microbes, or **microscopic organisms,**

Ginseng for sale in South Korea. Some people use plant products to help build up their resistance to disease. There is some evidence that certain plants such as ginseng can make white blood cells stronger.

such as bacteria and viruses. White blood cells do this by making chemicals that kill the organisms and destroy any toxins (poisons) the organisms may produce. The foreign chemicals are called **antigens.** The chemicals that the white blood cells make to attack them are called **antibodies.** Often these antibodies will stay in the bloodstream for many years after the antigen has been removed. If the same antigen attacks again, the body will be ready for it. The body has been made **immune** from attack.

In spite of the general efficiency of the white blood cells, some antigens slip past them and cause disease. They can do this if the person is not completely healthy or if the antigen has changed since the last time it invaded the person's body. Colds and flu viruses, for example, change their outer covering frequently, causing the body's **immune system** not to recognize them. Some viruses, such as the virus that causes AIDS (the HIV virus) and some that can cause cancer, get into the genetic instructions of the cells. The virus can hide there until it is triggered and begins to develop. One of the reasons that HIV is so dangerous is that it can pass from person to person while it hides in the cells. Another reason that HIV is so deadly is that it attacks the immune system leaving the body without any defenses at all. The best thing to do against these kinds of disease is to give the white blood cells immunity so that they are ready for attack.

Vaccination: a shield against disease

Your immune system has probably been made ready for some attacks with **vaccines,** which you either swallowed or were given as injections. Vaccines are made from bits of an organism that causes disease, either a virus such as measles or polio, or bacteria such as tetanus. The white blood cells clear away the vaccine by producing antibodies against it. These antibodies stay in your blood, so if the live organism attacks in the future, your body already has the antibodies for defense.

Vaccination against disease has been very successful. For example, in the 1970s smallpox, one of the most deadly diseases, was wiped out

THE WHITE KNIGHTS AT WORK

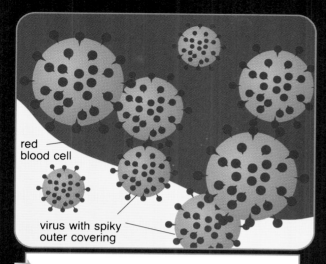

red blood cell

virus with spiky outer covering

1 A virus enters the blood stream.

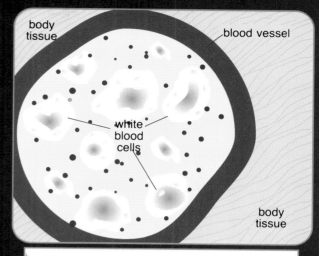

body tissue

blood vessel

white blood cells

body tissue

2 White cells come into contact with the virus.

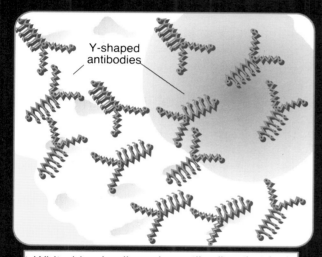

Y-shaped antibodies

3 White blood cells make antibodies that lock onto the spiky covering on the virus.

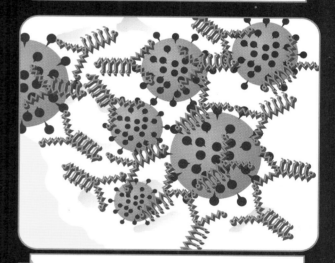

4 The viruses are trapped by the antibodies.

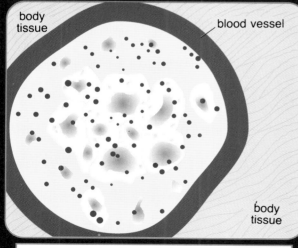

body tissue

blood vessel

body tissue

5 White blood cells and viruses are concentrated in lumps. Viruses are inactive.

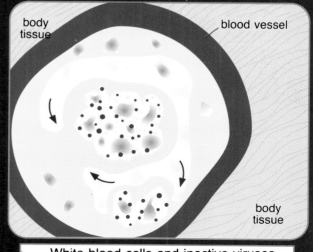

body tissue

blood vessel

body tissue

6 White blood cells and inactive viruses are cleared away by larger white cells

completely. Even when rewards of $1,000 were offered for reporting a case, none was found. The fight against this disease was a great success, but many of the world's poor are not vaccinated regularly enough to fight other major diseases. Their medical services often do not have enough staff, money, or vaccines to vaccinate all the children who need it. There are also other problems. For example, to be effective the vaccine against measles must be given when a baby is nine months old. By this time many of the babies will have caught the disease from adults and died from it. Some other vaccines, like that for polio, are not very useful in poor countries. Only about six out of 10 children are made immune. Nobody yet knows why. Even so, vaccination is the cheapest and best defense against disease in all countries. It gives the body's own white knights the weapons to fight disease for themselves.

Shielding the world
In 1984 three quarters of all the children of Colombia (over 10 million children) were vaccinated in three days. This shows what can be done when time, organization—and, above all, money—is put to the task. Nearly all the diseases in the list on page 7 have vaccines against them. If a worldwide effort, like that of Colombia's in 1984, were made today, the

numbers of people suffering from these diseases would shrink immediately. To buy vaccines for the world's poor countries would cost about 500 million dollars a year. This may seem like a lot, but compare it to some other figures. Every year in the United States people spend over 90 billion dollars on tobacco and alcohol (which are in any case sources of ill health). They also spend 20 billion dollars on children's toys. Costumes and candy for Halloween cost 800 million dollars. Other rich countries also spend enormous amounts on similar items. For example, people in England spend three and a half billion pounds on candy.

You can see that for these countries, the cost of vaccines would really be quite cheap. However, to poor countries with little spare money it could be very expensive. To protect the world from disease is a choice for the people of rich countries. If they were determined to do it, the money could easily be found.

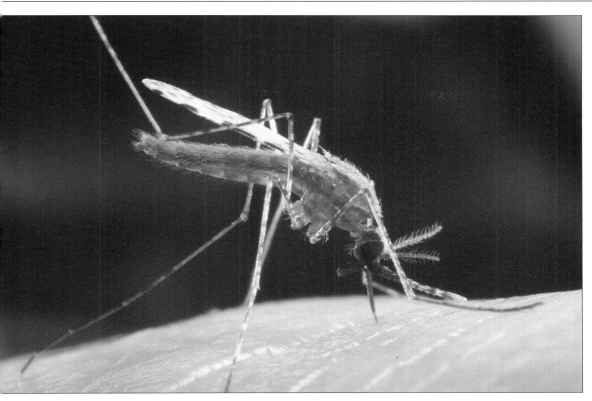

Developing new defenses

There are many diseases that have no vaccines against them. To develop new vaccines will cost money. But we must develop new vaccines soon. Many diseases are on the march!

AIDS is the best known at present but there are others. Dengue fever, for example, is carried by mosquitoes and has spread from South America into the Caribbean region. It has even reached the southern part of the United States. It was carried here by mosquitoes breeding in water trapped in old car tires imported from South America. Mosquitoes transfer the infection when they bite people. Malaria, another disease spread by mosquitoes, is also becoming established in new areas. Along the Mediterranean coastlines of France, Spain, and Italy sand flies now are infected with lieshmaniasis, a disease that can kill people.

As people travel around the world, diseases can be brought into new areas. Many people in England travel to Ghana. Each year two out of every 100 travelers return with a very lethal form of malaria. Fortunately, the malaria microbe cannot complete its life cycle in the cooler climate of England. But now England's climate is getting warmer. For many reasons it would benefit everyone, in poor countries or rich countries, to do all that is possible to prevent diseases throughout the world.

Fit for Thought?
● Find out which diseases you have been vaccinated against.

bacteria – tiny organisms. A few cause diseases but they can be treated with antibiotic medicines. (See glossary on page 44.)

viruses – tiny organisms that can cause disease. They cannot be treated with antibiotics.

microscopic organisms – tiny plants and animals that can only be seen through a microscope.

antigen – any chemical that causes antibodies to be produced.

antibody – a chemical that fights disease and is produced by some white blood cells.

immune – protected against infection by antibodies in the bloodstream.

immune system – the system by which white blood cells make antibodies and protect the body against infection.

vaccine – a substance made from dead viruses or bacteria, which gives immunity to disease when taken into the bloodstream.

Magic Bullets

In the last century the great German chemist Ehrlich was searching for a cure to the deadly disease called anthrax. He said he was looking for a "magic bullet," that is, a chemical that would kill the disease but not harm the patient. This is still the aim of drug designers today. However, most drugs have side effects: they harm the patient as well as the disease. About five out of every 100 people in the hospital are there because of the effects of the drugs they took to cure them. Even so, the search for "magic bullets"—drugs without side effects—still goes on.

Counting the cost

Thousands of drugs are in use today. About half of them come from plants. The rest have been designed and manufactured in a laboratory. Even these **synthetic drugs** may once have come from plants. Aspirin, the world's most widely-used drug, was first made from the bark of the willow tree. All drugs are tested on animals and on people before they are allowed to be sold. Many thousands of drugs are tried and rejected. Only a few survive the tests.

A machine operator checks pills on the production line.

Testing drugs. Blood from the horseshoe crab is used to test for toxins (poisons) in drugs. The crab is returned to the sea after some blood has been taken, but this weakens the animal and many die.

Testing drugs to make sure they are safe costs a great deal of money. In the United States it costs around 100 million dollars to test just one drug. To get this money back, the drug companies may have to charge a high price for the drug. The drug will be even more expensive if it is to be used against a rare disease. The high price of drugs is one of the reasons why health care in the rich countries costs more and more. In 1965 the United States spent about 6 percent of its wealth on health care (41.9 billion dollars). By 1990 the country was spending nearly 12 percent (over 500 billion dollars) on health care. Other rich countries, such as England, showed the same kind of growth in spending, although the total amount of money was not so great. This spending growth has begun to affect other needs including education, housing, and transportation. It has also left less money to help poor countries to become healthier. Many people are now asking that ways be found to reduce the amount of money spent on health care in rich countries.

Three main ways have been suggested to reduce the drugs bill. The first is to develop a healthier life-style and prevent illness in the first place. The second is to look for other sources for drugs in nature's own chemistry set. The third is to design drugs that aim very precisely at specific chemical targets to correct faulty chemistry. These would be the true 'magic bullets'' that Ehrlich was looking for. The first solution is available to anybody if they want it. (See pages 36–41.) The second solution has been available for thousands of years but only now is science beginning to take it seriously. The third solution is now being developed with the aid of the computer.

Drugs from plants

In 1400 B.C. in a temple at Karnak in Syria, the priests asked the temple builders to carve on the walls pictures of plants they used in medicine. There were more than 100 such plants. Even now three quarters of the world's population mainly use plants to fight disease. (See photographs on page 20.) Altogether about 20,000 different plant and animal products are used worldwide in traditional medicine. Scientists in many countries are analyzing these products to see what useful chemicals they contain. In eastern Asia over 350 different plants are used to treat diabetes. (This disease upsets the body's ability to use sugar properly.) In tests, some of these plants have been shown to be very effective. They include cinnamon root, certain plantain leaves, and some kinds of grasses.

Plants for people. Aristolochia, or pipe vine, (left) has been used in China to treat diabetes (but see below). Chemicals from the rosy periwinkle (inset), found in Madagascar, have been used to make a drug to treat childhood leukemia (blood cancer). A chemical in goosegrass (below, magnified), a common hedgerow plant in England, has been used to treat psoriasis (a skin disease).

Riches in the rain forest (right). Plants in the rain forest could provide cures for many kinds of diseases. Some people already use plant medicines (on sale in a market in Ecuador, inset) but many plants have not yet been tested.

Some plants have proved to be only partly effective and some have been found to be highly dangerous. One plant used in China and Korea, called aristolochia, was quite useful in treating diabetes. However, it also contains the most powerful cancer-forming chemical ever discovered. This connection had never been made by the traditional healers of China and Korea. There are many people in rich countries who believe that ''natural cures'' are better than our scientifically-designed drugs. The example of aristolochia shows that all that is ''natural'' is not necessarily good. Plant medicines may be very good but it is better to test them first.

Scientific development of plant drugs has already given us very useful (and fairly cheap) medicines. For instance, many patients who need a **general anesthetic** before an operation are given a substance first used by the Indians of the Amazon forests to catch monkeys. This is *curare,* which is obtained from a tree bark. The Indians tip their arrows and blowpipe darts with it. If the arrow or dart hits a monkey in the treetops, the *curare* completely relaxes all its muscles and it falls from the tree. In the operating room this muscle-relaxing property ensures that the patient's muscles will not move when the surgeon is operating.

Saving trees, saving life

Tests are being carried out not only on plants that are already in use, but also on plants that have never been tried before. Many of these "new" plants are in the tropical forests of South America, Asia, and Africa. The forests of Africa are rich in chemicals that work not only against viruses, bacteria, and fungi, but also against **parasites** such as worms that get into the body through the skin, or when people drink polluted water. These parasites cause much disease in tropical lands.

Sadly, many tropical forests have already been destroyed, so we will never know what useful chemicals they contained. The forest of Korup National Park, in the Cameroon in West Africa, remains intact and gives us some idea of how important trees could be for our future. One kind of tree, for example, contains a chemical that is highly effective against cancer cells. The chemical is too complex to make in a factory, so the tree will have to be the factory. But, even in protected areas like this national park, cutting trees for timber and to grow crops still goes on. The wood is used mainly in rich countries for furniture. A race is on between the developers who want to cut down the forest and the chemists who want to save them for making drugs. If the rich countries stopped using so much tropical hardwood timber, everyone would benefit in the long run. Who knows if some special wood in your house might have come from a tree containing something that one day could have saved your life.

One country, China, which cannot afford expensive drugs for its 1.2 billion people, wants to make most of its medicines from plants. The Institute of Medicinal Plant Medicine has been set up in Beijing and the forests are protected by law, so the plants are preserved. In the twenty-first century the same steps will probably be taken by other countries. Already the United States and England are sending expeditions to the tropical forests to find out from the local people how they use the plants as medicines. There is no doubt that as science digs into nature's huge storehouse of plant (and animal) chemicals, many more "magic bullets" will be discovered.

Chemistry by computer

In the laboratories that research and make drugs, hit-and-miss methods of finding new drugs are now being replaced by very precise drug-designing. The process is rather like designing a weapon. Just as a weapon designer needs to know exactly what sort of target the weapon is meant to destroy, so a drug designer needs to know the target for the new drug.

The first stage in designing a drug is to find out exactly what the chemical is like that is causing the illness and where its weak points are. Very often the chemicals that cause illness are proteins. These are large chemicals and usually very complicated.

First the chemists must break down the protein bit by bit and analyze the pieces. The computer uses X-ray pictures to build up a three-dimensional picture of the protein (see photograph below). From this picture, the drug designer can work out where there may be a chemical link in the protein, into which a new drug could lock. If the drug is successful, it upsets the balance of chemicals in the protein, and the activity of the protein may then be stopped completely. It is rather like adding an extra card to a house of cards: the extra card causes the whole structure to collapse.

So far there are few such drugs in use. One that is likely to come into wide use soon is designed to interfere with a protein called renin which causes high blood pressure. Before the next century there are likely to be many designed drugs in use for many conditions. The techniques developed for designing drugs may also provide better vaccines. The body's own white knights will be given much more precise weapons to fight such diseases as HIV, the common cold, and flu. We will then be able to make our own "magic bullets."

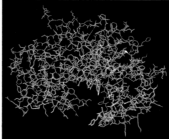

Computer graphics. This is a computer picture of the protein renin.

Sea squirts and other soft-bodied marine animals (see page 10) produce chemicals that protect them from being eaten. One sea squirt contains a chemical that has been used to treat leukemia and skin cancer.

A beekeeper removing a
honeycomb from a hive.

A honeybee collecting
pollen.

More than a Sweetener

Not every natural cure comes from plants. For thousands of years the
honeybee has provided one of the best natural medicines in the world.
Honey contains many chemicals other than sugars. These chemicals
are useful in healing wounds, and helping to cure stomach upsets and
diarrhea caused by bacteria.

Honeycomb wax is glued together by a substance, called propolis,
made by bees. Propolis has a strong antiseptic action and is one of the
reasons hives are so clean. It is present in the honey we eat and recent
research shows that it may have anti-cancer properties as well.

Honey may also be useful to anybody who suffers from hay fever.
Bees use large amounts of pollen to make honey. A spoonful of honey
taken each day for the year before the start of the hay-fever season—
especially if the honey is local—allows the body to build up a defense
against the effects of the pollen.

Fit for Thought?
- From a library book of herbal cures find out
  for what illnesses these common plants
  can be used: garlic, parsley, sage, thyme,
  elderberry, marigold, raspberry, mint,
  stinging nettle, rhubarb.
  Some of these plants contain chemicals
  that can affect our own chemistry.

synthetic drugs – drugs made in the
laboratory.
general anesthetic – a drug that makes the
whole body temporarily lose feeling.
parasites – plants and animals that live in or
on other organisms and take their food from
these organisms.
antiseptic – able to stop bacteria growth.

Technology for Tomorrow

In 1989 medical engineers in Scotland developed a tiny sewing machine for surgery. It is so small it can be swallowed. If a patient has a bleeding stomach ulcer the machine will stitch up the wound. It is directed from outside the patient's body by a surgeon using a scanner to see what is going on. This machine is typical of the most advanced medicine today. Pacemakers that regulate the heartbeat and artificial joints that allow people to move more easily are quite common in rich countries. Many of the materials used to make these implants were developed for use in the NASA space program. Others have been adapted from materials used in the electronics industry.

New materials are being discovered and adapted all the time. In the 1980s it was discovered by accident that if certain kinds of plastic had small amounts of chemicals such as iodine added to them, they would conduct electricity. Since then, chemists have been searching for a material that could be used in the body to replace nerves, which carry electrical messages from the brain. We can expect to see new materials being used by the end of the century to make artificial nerves. The great hope is that people who are paralyzed because their nerves are damaged might be able to move their bodies again by using artificial nerves.

The technology of healing is now one of the world's most advanced industries. Just as advanced engineering went into outer space, it

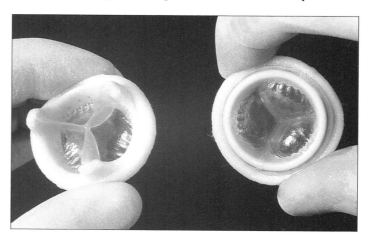

Using new materials (above) These artificial valves, for connecting the heart to the main blood vessel, are made from very advanced new materials.

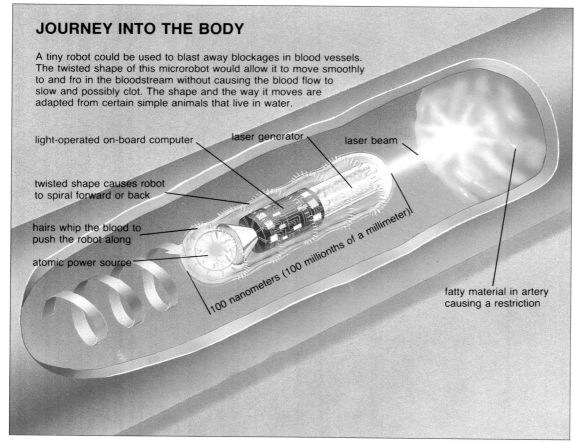

JOURNEY INTO THE BODY

A tiny robot could be used to blast away blockages in blood vessels. The twisted shape of this microrobot would allow it to move smoothly to and fro in the bloodstream without causing the blood flow to slow and possibly clot. The shape and the way it moves are adapted from certain simple animals that live in water.

light-operated on-board computer

laser generator

laser beam

twisted shape causes robot to spiral forward or back

hairs whip the blood to push the robot along

atomic power source

100 nanometers (100 millionths of a millimeter)

fatty material in artery causing a restriction

will now explore the inner space of the body. At Tokyo University a sort of inner-space ship is being developed. It is a microrobot designed to travel on its own through the spaces between the tissues. It measures only millionths of a millimeter (nanometers), which is the size of the spaces between the tissues of the body. It will have its own power source and tiny computer. It will also have a sort of laser chisel to clear blockages from arteries and veins. When it is produced it will be very expensive, but if it works, the twenty-first century will see many more equally complex machines doing jobs inside us.

Seeing more clearly

Until very recently the only way of seeing inside a patient was to open up the body or to use X rays. Both of these methods can be dangerous. Now there are new ways of seeing inside the body without an operation. One method is to use scanners. Scanners use different kinds of energy sources to penetrate the body: for instance, sound waves (ultra-sound scanners), magnetism (NMR scanners), and heat given off by diseased tissues (thermal **tomography**). X rays are still used, but when

they are used for scanning, a rapid series of pictures is built up by a computer into a three-dimensional diagram. This is called CAT scanning (Computer-Aided Tomography). (Photographs of some of these methods are shown on these pages.) Another way of seeing inside the body, which may have even more possibilities for the future, is to use an endoscope. An endoscope is a sort of internal telescope. Most endoscopes are made of thin fibers of glass, which are very flexible. Light can be sent along these fibers. There is a microscope at one end so the doctor can look down and see part of the patient's body. The image can also be shown on a screen, or it can even be photographed. Although the fibers are already thinner than a human hair, in the future they are likely to be much finer. They will be only millionths of a millimeter thick. Then they may be able to carry tiny instruments that will measure what is going on chemically, even inside individual cells.

All these developments are, of course, very expensive and so far there are few of them in the poor countries of the world. In 1990 there were more than 500 NMR scanners in the United States, but fewer than 20 in Africa.

A baby rests on a water bed over an ultrasound scanner (left).

A CAT scanner (below).

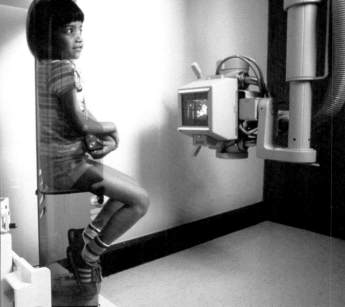

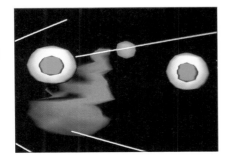

Thermal tomography (right). A tumor between the eyes shows up as red on the heat scanner.

A "barefoot doctor" in China.

Barefoot doctors

Some poor countries have designed health care systems to make the best use of the resources they have. In China and Tanzania, for example, much of the health care is not done by doctors at all. "Barefoot doctors" are trained to visit villages and deal with many illnesses without themselves being qualified as doctors. They are called "barefoot" because in the past only the fully qualified doctors could afford to buy shoes. Barefoot doctors have a carefully designed list of **symptoms.** By following this list they can decide whether to treat the illness with the medicines they carry. If the symptoms do not fit the symptom chart, the patient may be sent on to a medical center where better equipment may be available. If the illness cannot be cured there, the patient may be sent to a local hospital. Only then will the patient see any sort of modern health technology. In poor countries one of the most important pieces of medical technology is often the bicycle!

Computer-aided design

The computer is being used more and more in medicine, to do all kinds of jobs. We have already seen how it is used to design new drugs. (See page 22.) Computer-aided design is also being used to make new artificial spare parts. In the United States, new hip joints are made in hospital workshops according to designs specified by computer. The designs are based on an analysis of pictures from scanners of the exact shape of the patient's joints. Another use has been developed to help children who cannot walk because of an inherited condition such as cerebral palsy. The computer is given information from scanners about the limbs and joints. It then guides the surgeon to rearrange the muscles and nerves in the

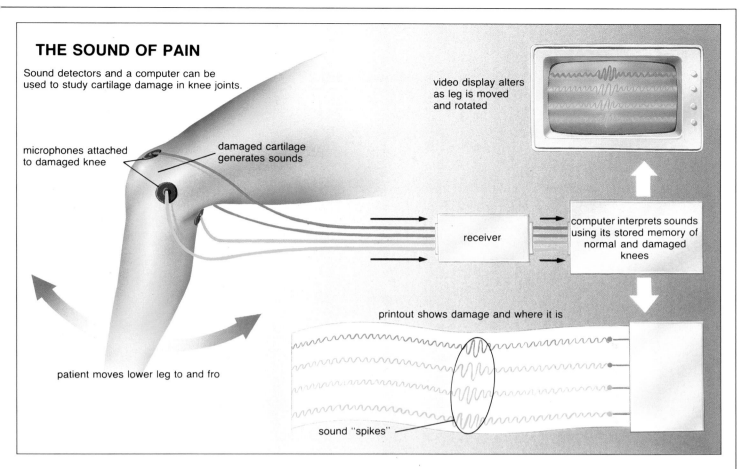

THE SOUND OF PAIN

Sound detectors and a computer can be used to study cartilage damage in knee joints.

microphones attached to damaged knee

damaged cartilage generates sounds

video display alters as leg is moved and rotated

receiver

computer interprets sounds using its stored memory of normal and damaged knees

patient moves lower leg to and fro

printout shows damage and where it is

sound "spikes"

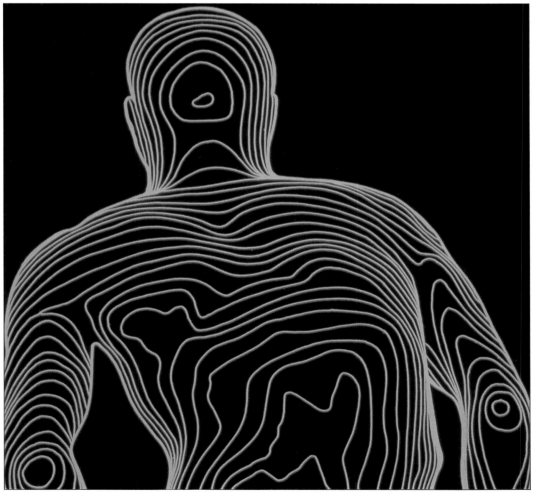

Body map. A computer has been used to build up a contour map of a man's back. The doctor can use the map to measure how far the spine has been deformed by polio.

legs. Children who would otherwise be in a wheelchair all their lives are now walking, thanks to the skill of the surgeon who is aided by the scanners, endoscopes, and computers of modern medical technology.

In England, computer analysis of ordinary X-ray pictures of limb bones has been developed to estimate the thinning of bone in older women. The thinning (called osteoporosis) is due to a loss of calcium from the bones and is the cause of many fractures from falls. The computer can analyze the X rays and estimate the amount of calcium in the bones. From this the doctor can recommend extra calcium treatment to make up for the loss.

Consulting the computer
As computers become cheaper, they will be of increasing value in the poor countries where there are not enough doctors. The computer can store huge amounts of information about symptoms. As talking computers are developed perhaps even quite poor villages will be able to buy one to act as a first "mechanical doctor." Patients will be able to consult the computer and get immediate answers in their own language. The computer may also be programmed to pass on information about a patient to a barefoot doctor, nurse, or hospital doctor if it is determined that the illness needs more attention.

Talking computers are already being used in the United States to reduce costs for the patient. The system may well become more widespread in other rich countries. In England it is estimated that well over half the visits made to doctors are for minor illnesses, which could be dealt with by the patient or treated in a routine way. Only a small number of visits are for really serious conditions that need the attention of a fully-qualified doctor. The computer could look after many of the minor illnesses, leaving the doctor free to care for more serious cases. A patient could telephone the computer at any time of day or night, which would save the patient's time as well as the doctor's.

The gentle art of surgery
About a century ago, the outcome from surgery for patients was simple—be killed or be cured. Those days are long gone, but surgery still carries some risks to the patient. It is also a very expensive form of treatment, which usually needs nursing care. Surgeons are trying to reduce the costs and the dangers of surgery.

As scanners improve there is less and less need to open up the patient to see what is going on inside. Many operations are now carried out using scanners, endoscopes, and thin tubes, called catheters, shaped to reach particular organs or parts of organs like the heart, liver, and kidneys. Catheters can carry tiny instruments at their tip, such as cutters, tweezers, and even pressure jets, which can be used to blast away blockages in arteries. At Kiel University hospital in northern Germany, the technique of "keyhole surgery" is being developed. The surgeon simply makes tiny holes in the body, through which endoscopes and catheters are passed. The cutting, sewing, and removal of diseased tissue is controlled from outside the body by the surgeon. Another technique, especially for heart surgery, is being carried out at Guy's Hospital in London. Special catheters are introduced into the large vein in the upper leg and passed to the heart. The catheters can carry new valves, and patches of a special material to cover holes in the heart muscles and blood vessels. They can also be used to cut and sew damaged parts and clear blockages. Surgeons in this hospital believe that by 2020, heart surgery will be as routine and safe as a visit to the dentist.

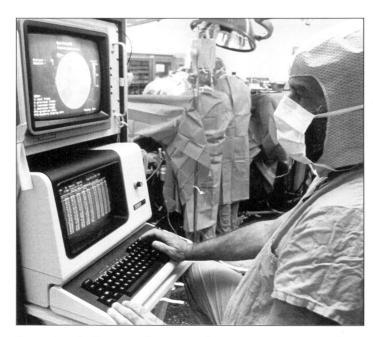

Computers in the operating room. A surgeon uses a computer during an operation on the brain.

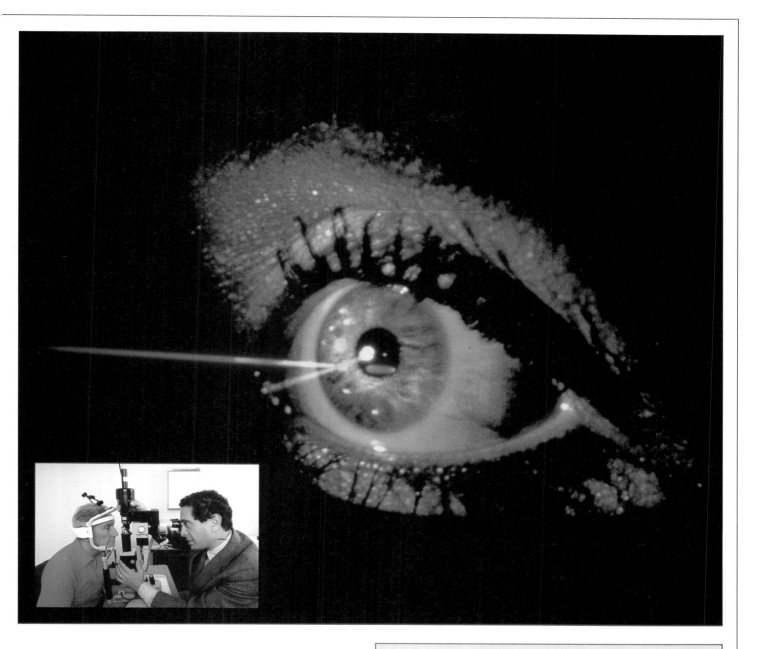

Lasers at work. The patient's head is held steady in a brace (inset) and a laser beam is aimed at the eye to precisely burn away damaged tissue.

Perhaps one of the biggest advantages of such developments is that although they are expensive to develop, in the long run they cut costs. Not only are the operations cheaper, but the time a patient has to spend in the hospital is reduced. This makes resources free for other uses. As we have seen, one of the most important points to consider in choosing to aim for "Health for all by 2000" is the cost. Only by using modern technology will this be possible. If the costs of medical treatment are cut in rich countries it will free many more resources to aid those countries that still have far to go to provide even basic medical care.

Fit for Thought?
- Work out a list of questions that you think a computer might ask a patient in order to diagnose a cold, flu, or another common illness.
- Imagine that you feel unwell. At the doctor's office you have to consult a computer. What would be the advantages and disadvantages of such a system?

tomography – producing computer-aided three-dimensional pictures of part of the body.
symptoms – signs of a disease.

Hazards on the Road to Health

In the first chapter we saw that the three foundations for a healthy life are clean water, good drains and sewage systems, and good food. We also know that these cost money and that most money comes from modern industries in rich countries. Although industry is creating the wealth for a healthy life it is also creating the conditions that can damage health. It does this first by the dangers from working in industry and second by its products.

Danger at work

All industries have hazards from the machines and processes used to make things. In rich countries there are usually strong laws to protect people from the worst hazards of industry, although accidents are not prevented unless employer and employee follow the safety rules. (In poor countries there may be hardly any rules at all to protect the workers.) When the rules are not followed, the damage may be very great not only to the workers but to others as well. The Chernobyl nuclear accident in the Soviet Union was caused by workers ignoring safety standards. The accident is now affecting as many as two million people. Large areas of the country will have to be sealed off for decades because of radioactive fallout from the fire in the nuclear reactor.

The dangers from the products of industry are affecting everyone's health. In this case, the laws and regulations are much weaker than those that control working methods and conditions in factories, farms, and offices.

Sellafield nuclear reprocessing plant in Cumbria, England. Nuclear power stations generate waste. At present there is no safe way of disposing of these wastes, so they are kept underwater in ponds (inset).

Accident in Bolivia. In developing countries poor roads are often the cause of accidents.

Taking risks

Some industrial products such as tobacco are obviously dangerous. Every day thousands of people die from diseases caused by smoking tobacco. The danger is clear—tobacco is a killer. Fortunately, many young people realize this and do not smoke. And others who have smoked for years are quitting. This is good news. But the reduced sales have prompted tobacco companies to sell cigarettes in poor countries where, until now, few people smoked. The people in poor countries have enough health hazards without adding this one.

Another industrial product less obviously dangerous is the automobile. We can do without a dangerous product like tobacco, but can we manage without cars or other forms of transportation? Most of us travel in cars, airplanes, trains, or motorcycles (the most dangerous form of transportation), without giving much thought to the risks. We use complex machinery and electrical equipment and accept the risks for the sake of convenience. However, as the world becomes more complex and we depend more on machines, the chances for accidents increase.

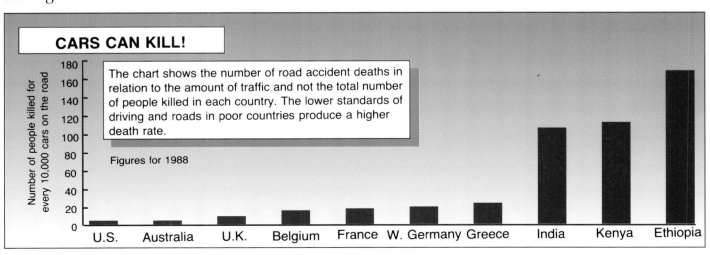

CARS CAN KILL!

Number of people killed for every 10,000 cars on the road

The chart shows the number of road accident deaths in relation to the amount of traffic and not the total number of people killed in each country. The lower standards of driving and roads in poor countries produce a higher death rate.

Figures for 1988

U.S.   Australia   U.K.   Belgium   France   W. Germany   Greece   India   Kenya   Ethiopia

Polluted playgrounds. The children in Colombia (left) and the boy in England (right) are all playing in water polluted by factory wastes.

A messy world

Modern industry and farming create the products that give us our wealth. Unfortunately, they also add to our environment substances that are either directly harmful to health or can be harmful to some people. These substances are generally called pollutants. A pollutant is any substance added to the natural environment that interferes with the environment. Pollutants can be in the form of waste gases, liquids, or solids poured into the air and sea or dumped on land. Many of these are directly harmful as they are toxic (poisonous).

The lead used in gasoline in western Europe is a good example of a harmful pollutant. It is especially harmful to the brain and nervous system of young children. It is also harmful to many kinds of wild and cultivated plants. At one stage in the 1970s in the United States, the levels of lead in forests far away from major roads were rising so rapidly that the plants were in danger of being killed off. It was realized that the lead was carried in the air and then washed into the soil by rain. The federal government then banned lead in gasoline. Since then, rain has washed most of the lead from the soil.

The removal of lead from gasoline has reduced one health hazard, but toxic pollution from other metals continues to increase. Every year the countries around the North Sea pour hundreds of tons of metal wastes into their rivers. They also pollute the water with toxic metals and dangerous chemicals. As the rivers flow into the sea, the pollutants are absorbed by small floating marine plants. The plants are consumed by animals, including fish that are eventually eaten by people.

The worst pollution of water is close to the shores of industrial countries, especially in nearly enclosed seas like the Irish Sea, the Black Sea, the Baltic, the Mediterranean, and the Inland Sea of Japan. But the pollution does not stay there. It spreads throughout the oceans so that all seas are now contaminated. Seals and whales in the Arctic have been found to have high levels of pollutants in their bodies. Some of them even die from these poisons. The Inuit (Eskimos) who eat these animals find that the pollutants build up in their bodies, which can affect their health.

In areas near factories, the effects of pollutants on health can be very serious. In the most polluted place in the world, Silesia in Poland, air pollution produces chronic breathing problems in three quarters of all 10-year-old children. The children are also small for their age. In fact, it is children who are the most likely to be harmed by pollution. Even with fairly clean air and water, changes in children's health can be seen. Childhood asthma, for example, is increasing in England. At present, we do not know the exact cause of this but it is likely to be an effect of pollution. So even "clean" countries like England, which have reduced the worst effects of air and water pollution, must not think they have solved all the health problems caused by pollution. As we produce more and more wastes, we will have to spend more and more money to make sure the wastes are kept under control.

Polluted air over Moscow, U.S.S.R. Smoke from power plants and industry pollutes the air in many countries in Europe, in the United States, and in China.

Good food?

Most people in rich countries now have a diet on which they can stay healthy. However, in order to produce enough food at a reasonable price, large amounts of chemicals are used to increase food production. These include herbicides (weed killers), pesticides (insect killers), fungicides (fungus killers), and fertilizers. This **intensive farming** has been very successful in producing large quantities of food but there is a pollution cost. The chemicals may be washed into rivers and pollute the water. In fact, sometimes farming pollutes rivers and groundwater more than industry does.

Many of the chemicals sprayed on soil and plants to control pests and diseases are still present in the food when we eat it. Food that goes from farm to factory to be processed has more chemicals added to preserve, color, and flavor it. Many people see these chemicals as pollutants as well.

Of course, all the chemicals are tested to see if they are safe to eat. But there is no guarantee that nobody will be affected by them. Research in the United States, Canada, and England suggests that children's behavior and even their school results are affected by modern processed

foods. Experiments have shown that removing additives from food produced improvements in both behavior and school performance. For reasons like this and because they are worried by modern farming methods, many people in rich countries are choosing to alter their diets. In England more people are switching to organic foods, grown without artificial fertilizers and crop sprays. Many people are also becoming vegetarian. In 1990 one survey in England showed that about two million people were completely vegetarian and another three and a half million seldom ate meat.

In the United States the change of diet is even more striking. In the 1960s and 70s farmers borrowed lots of money to buy the machinery to use the new agricultural chemicals. The chemicals greatly increased the yields of the few crops the farmers grew. So much extra food was produced that the prices fell and farmers found it very hard to pay their debts. As a result some farmers are changing back to older farming methods: They use animal fertilizers, cut down on chemicals, and grow a bigger variety of crops. Many of these farmers are even abandoning chemicals altogether and growing more organic food. As the American consumer

Spraying orange trees in the United States. Some people prefer untreated fruit.

Return of a Killer

Are cars the culprit? Vehicle fumes may have been the cause of the increase in childhood asthma in the 1980s.

In December 1952 the Great London Smog killed more than 2,000 people. Many of the victims suffered from asthma, in which the small tubes in the lungs swell from irritation by smoke, dust, or any chemical to which the person is allergic. (An allergy is an overreaction by the immune system to a substance.) Breathing becomes very difficult and the attack may be fatal in severe cases. In the days of open coal fires the peak for asthma was in winter when coal smoke was at its worst.

After the Great Smog, the Clean Air Act was passed by Parliament in 1958. Conditions in the cities began to improve and for a while asthma became less common. However, since 1980 the number of cases has doubled. Instead of being at a maximum in winter as before, the peak for attacks is now in summer. Doctors have decided that now the asthma might be caused not by coal smoke but by photochemical smog.

Photochemical smog is created as chemicals from car exhausts are acted on by sunlight. All kinds of pollutants are formed, but one—ozone—is especially poisonous. The doctors reasoned that the increased number of cars combined with the series of sunny summers during the last decade had provided the right conditions.

There are other possible reasons why asthma is on the increase. More chemical sprays have been used on fields in the last ten years. The sprays can drift for miles. There may also be allergic responses to new chemicals added in increasing amounts to foods. Only more research will prove exactly what is happening. Medical research of this kind will be increasingly important in the future as the connections between health and the environment are investigated.

becomes more health-conscious, the demand for organic food is rising. By 2020 at least half the food sold will probably be organic.

By that time genetic engineers may have developed new crops able to resist diseases and pests for themselves and needing much less fertilizer to give good yields and good profits.

Cleaning up the mess

Many organizations are dedicated to cleaning up our messy environment. Their influence is growing all the time as more and more people decide they want a better future for their children. The modern science of **ecology** has taught us that every living part of the planet is connected to every other part. People are connected by water, air, and the food they eat. If we pollute the system, eventually the pollution will harm us by one or another of these routes. We can ignore the danger for a while but we cannot hide from it forever.

Fit for Thought?
- In your kitchen cabinets or refrigerator there will be many cans and packages of food. Look at the labels and try to find which ingredients are food and which are the chemicals added to it. Make a list of these chemicals and try to find out why they have been added to the product.
- What steps would you take as a parent to ensure the healthy upbringing of your family?

intensive farming – the use of modern methods and chemicals to efficiently produce large quantities of food.
ecology – the study of how plants, animals, and people are related to their environment.

Prescription for Health

In the 1970s the number of people in the United States who died an early death caused by a heart attack began to fall as people realized that they could avoid heart attacks by cutting out smoking, reducing fats in the diet, and getting more exercise. As people in rich countries become aware of how their state of health depends on how they live, they are choosing more sensible lifestyles.

You are what you eat

"You are digging your grave with your teeth!" was once the doctor's cry to the patient. It is just as true today that people damage their health by eating the wrong foods. A study in Britain in the 1980s compared the diets and ways of life of men in northern Britain—the heart attack "capital" of the world—with those in southern Britain, where the heart attack rate is much lower. After carefully matching people for smoking, exercise, and type of work, the researchers concluded that the most important difference was that men in the south of England ate more fresh fruit and vegetables than those in the north. Similar conclusions had already been reached in other countries. In fact, studies have shown that food plays a major part in causing many cancers as well as heart disease. Guidelines were issued in the United States in 1987 on "protective" foods. These foods may help the body's white knights fight or prevent both cancer and heart disease.

DIET AND DISEASE

These are some parts of the body that can be affected by eating too much or too little of certain foods.

Body part	Disease	Diet at fault	Diet to follow (as recommended by American medical authorities)
eyes	blindness cataracts	too little vitamin A	eat more green leafy vegetables, oily fish, fish oils, carrots
throat	cancer	too little vitamin A	
heart	heart disease	too much fat	reduce fat and use olive oil, eat more fruit
breast	cancer (in females)	too much fat and sugar	and vegetables
lungs	cancer	tobacco	stop smoking
stomach	cancer	smoked and pickled foods	eat less smoked and pickled food
pancreas	cancer (possibly diabetes)	too much fat	eat less fat
colon	cancer	too much fat and sugar, too little fiber	eat more whole wheat bread, fruit, vegetables, and oatmeal
ovaries	cancer (in females)	too much fat	eat less fat
prostate gland	cancer (in males)	too much fat	eat less fat

In general, cut down on animal fats, especially those in meats and dairy products. Olive oil should replace other cooking oils. Vitamins C and E should be increased. Food should not be overcooked and more raw food should be eaten. Vegetables such as sprouts, cabbage, cauliflower, and broccoli have a general "protective" quality.

Too much of a good thing

Of course it is not only the type of food eaten that affects people's health but also the amounts and how they are cooked. We know, for example, that we need much less protein—especially meat protein—to stay healthy than is usually eaten in rich countries. This was proved during World War II in England when the meat ration was reduced to only 8 ounces (225 grams) per week (the same as two hamburgers). Fats were rationed to 6 ounces (170 grams), sugar was reduced to 8 ounces (225 grams), and only two fresh eggs were allowed. Yet people stayed very healthy because bread, vegetables, fruit, and fish were not rationed. Much of the fresh food was produced organically. Children grew up well (they were given free milk at school) and did not suffer from more diseases on this diet. Their teeth were healthy, too, as it was almost impossible to buy chocolate and other sweets. In fact, because many poor people got a well-balanced diet for the first time, and because people walked much more and used bicycles, they became healthier than before the war. All the figures for measuring health, such as infant mortality, deaths from heart attacks, and cancer rates fell between 1939 and 1945. Many people may even have been healthier than their descendants are now, in wealthier, more peaceful times. One third of British adults are now overweight. Fat people are more likely to get heart and other diseases than slim people.

Too little of a good thing

Most diets in the world outside the rich countries are very like those of wartime England. In China, for example, meat is used only to flavor and give texture to the meal. In Africa most people are vegetarian most of the time. Where there are plenty of vegetables of different kinds, people are healthy. The difficulty for poor people in many tropical countries is getting enough nourishing food of any kind.

Staple foods such as bananas, cassava, corn, and plantains do not contain enough energy for children to grow strong and healthy. Fats such as peanut butter, margarine, and cooking oils, which do have the necessary energy, may be expensive and in short supply. The

Enough is as good as a feast. Some people in developing countries enjoy a varied, healthy diet, based on fish, vegetables, and fruit (left, in Thailand). Wartime rations in Britain (below left) provided a surprisingly healthy diet because red meat was scarce but vegetables and fruit were readily available. Today, most people in developed countries can choose their diet from a vast range of foods (below).

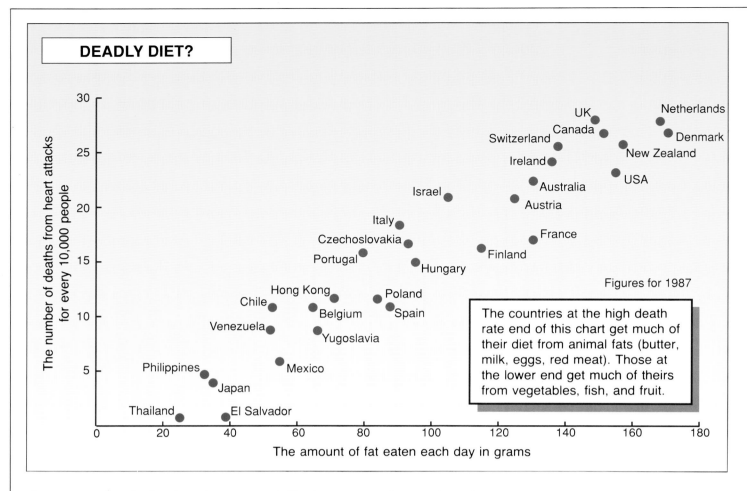

DEADLY DIET?

The number of deaths from heart attacks for every 10,000 people *(y-axis)*

The amount of fat eaten each day in grams *(x-axis)*

Figures for 1987

The countries at the high death rate end of this chart get much of their diet from animal fats (butter, milk, eggs, red meat). Those at the lower end get much of theirs from vegetables, fish, and fruit.

diet may also lack vitamins, especially in areas that have a long dry season, such as India and the grassy areas of Africa. In these areas a lack of vitamins can produce very serious diseases, particularly blindness. It is estimated that over 10,000 children lose their sight each year in India alone through lack of vitamin A. (One injection of vitamin A can protect against blindness for about six months. The cost of such an injection is just a few cents.)

A poor diet means that children are often smaller than children in rich countries. When they grow up, small mothers tend to produce underweight babies. The average 20-year-old Indian woman weighs around 16 percent less than a non-overweight woman of the same age in North America or western Europe. The smaller children born to these mothers cannot resist disease so well and so the cycle of poor health continues.

Mind over matter
When new drugs or treatments are to be tested, medical scientists use a special kind of test called a double-blind trial. In a test like this neither the doctors nor the patients

themselves know who is getting the drug. Half the patients get the real drug and half get a harmless substitute called a placebo. This group acts as a control for comparison with the drug-treated group. The effects of the drug can then be determined.

Only at the end of the test is it known which group of patients had the real drug. At this stage a surprising thing often happens. In the group that has had no drugs at all, a number of people, often quite a large number, will have been cured as well. They will have cured themselves because they believed they were taking the real medicine. Doctors call this the placebo effect. It is one of the most striking examples of the part our minds play in keeping us healthy. Many people have already begun to work out their own ways to use mind power to help fight disease. Doctors and scientists are only just beginning to see how effective mind power can be.

Using the power of the mind to cure illness is a very ancient skill. It is used today by many traditional societies around the world. For instance, the Navajo Indian healers have learned to recognize and treat more than 300 different physical and mental illnesses without modern drugs, using the patient's own mind power in various ways. The traditional ways of curing, such as dancing, story-telling, and making the patient sweat, may seem strange treatment to modern eyes. Yet they have been shown by research often to be very effective. Together with hypnosis and drugs made from local plants that can alter a person's mood, the rituals help the patients to fight the illness themselves. The aim is to restore harmony between the patient and the natural world.

We do not yet know scientifically how the placebo effect or the Navajo rituals work. Many doctors and scientists still need to be convinced that they can work as well as modern drugs. Only careful double-blind trials will persuade the medical profession of the power of the mind as a healer.

In 1990 British doctors announced the results of a 15-year experiment on women with the early stages of breast cancer. In 1975 women with the disease at one hospital were interviewed and then divided into three groups. The first group found the disease a big nuisance and wanted to get back to normal life as soon as possible. Another group saw the disease as something to fight. But a third group took the news badly and became depressed. At the end of the 15 years it was found that nearly half of the first two groups were still alive. All groups had had the same treatment at the same hospital. The only difference between the two groups with the better survival rate and the one with a poor survival rate was attitude. It seems that those patients willing to put up a fight gave themselves a better chance to defeat the disease. This kind of evidence will convince many doctors of the power of the mind.

Many people are already changing their ways of thinking in order to reduce the stresses and strains of modern life. Practices such as yoga, meditation, and relaxation techniques help to strengthen our abilities to resist disease. It may be that by the next century such techniques will be taught in schools as part of the preparation for adult life.

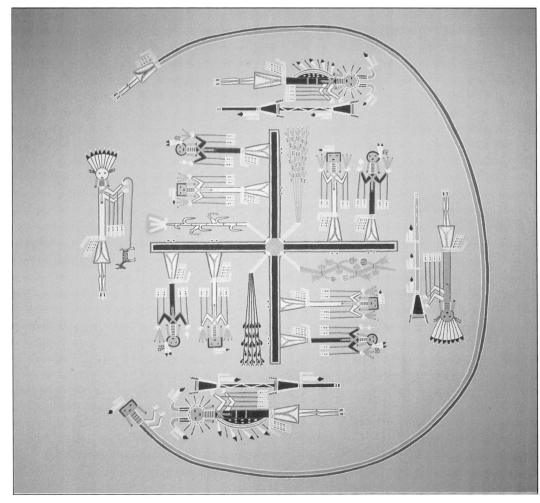

The whirling log. This sand picture, in powdered sandstone and charcoal, was made by a Navajo Indian medicine man. It shows four logs, each guarded by gods, around a lake. Pictures like this are made on the floor of a timber lodge during the annual eight-day "curing ceremonial," after which they are destroyed. This one is preserved in a museum.

Alternative Medicine

Some people use techniques such as these, many of which are thousands of years old, instead of, or as well as, modern medicine.

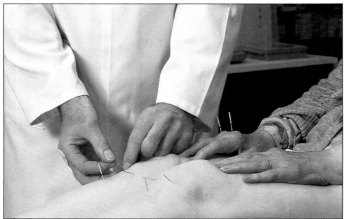

In **acupuncture (above)**, fine needles are pushed into the skin at certain places on the body to take away pain.

In **aromatherapy (left)**, oils from plants are rubbed into the skin to take away stress.

Yoga (below left) exercises may be used to take away stress.

In **reflexology (below)**, the feet are massaged to relieve pain in other parts of the body.

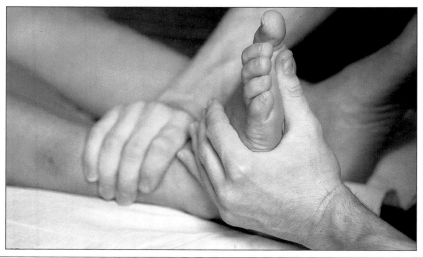

Evolution, exercise, and health

A study in 1990 showed that the hearts of many schoolchildren rarely reached their maximum rates of output. It is essential for future healthy hearts that maximum output should be reached frequently. Exercise for fitness is just as important for adults. Exercise not only strengthens the lungs and muscles but it also tones up the immune system. After about 10 minutes of continuous hard exercise—fast walking, running, cycling, swimming, and some ball games—the brain begins to release chemicals, called brain opiates. These are natural drug-like substances and have a calming effect on the brain. They also help the immune system to defend the body.

Sports are good for you! Children and adults need regular exercise in order to stay fit.

These helpful effects of hard exercise result from the kind of animal the human being is. We survived in the wild in the long-distant past not by being very strong or having big teeth, or by being fast runners. We survived because our brains were better than those of other animals at learning, communicating, and inventing new ways to live.

Exploring inner space
The brain plays a big part in keeping us healthy, yet, even now, we know very little about how it works. We can make maps of what happens in different parts of the brain. We do not yet know how these parts join together to make our "minds." In fact, we do not even have a clear idea of what we mean by a "mind" at all. Just as we have explored outer space in the last part of this century, in the next century we will be exploring the inner space of the brain and the mind. Many of the keys to a long healthy life lie within this complex, wonderful, and mysterious lump of gray matter.

Fit for Thought?
- Try this test of mind over matter. Imagine a cut lemon with juice oozing out of it. Is there a change in your mouth?
- Average maximum heart rate per minute is 220 less your age in years. The rate will vary around this figure for different individuals. Test your heart rate after a fast run or bicycle ride. Count the rate for six seconds and multiply by 10. A whole school class could do this and see what the variation is. How often does your heart rate reach its maximum? It should be at least three or four times a week.
- The thinking part of the brain, at the front, works in two halves. Ask a friend to think of a place he or she went on vacation. Watch the movement of his or her eyes. If they move to the right or left, this is the part of the brain being used to think about the question.
- Do you agree that our mind is "chemistry and wiring" as most scientists believe? Or is it something insubstantial that does not exist in a solid form?

A Long Life and a Healthy One

In the rich countries at least, many people now live longer than the 70 years given in the Bible as the human life span. In fact, nobody knows what the natural length of a human life should be. It has risen considerably in rich countries. An increasing number of people now reach 90 years and beyond. Much of this rise is due to how much is spent on looking after the old. However, it is also due to better conditions during the whole of people's lives.

The four stages of life

Sociologists (people who study society) say life can be divided into four stages. The first stage is childhood and adolescence, when we are learning. The second stage is our working life, during which we bring up our families. The third stage is when we are retired from work. Finally, there is the fourth stage of physical decline. The choice for health for the future will be to make the third stage as long as possible and the fourth stage as pain-free as possible. In poor countries there is rarely a third stage and even the first may be very short. Children either die or they start work very young.

The foundations for a long and healthy life lie in the first stage. On the whole, the healthier the childhood, the longer the life—unless there is an accident. One of the greatest achievements of this century has been finding out about what children need in order to grow and learn successfully. This does not mean only food. They need much more than this. The most important extras are to feel loved and secure and to see themselves as worthwhile people. Unloved children get ill more easily and do not grow or learn well. Happy children are usually good at learning and stay healthy. If the feeling of self-worth is well-established at home and school it forms the foundation for building a successful healthy life through the second stage.

Vitamins for vitality

In the 1960s, when Russian astronauts began to spend longer periods in space, doctors noticed that when they returned to earth their bodies showed changes similar to aging. In particular, they had produced a lot of active chemicals that were interfering with normal body chemistry. These chemicals (called free radicals) are produced in larger amounts as we get older. They are responsible, for example, for stiffening up the fibers that join our tissues together. This is one of the reasons why muscles and joints do not work so well as we age. It used to be thought that they were also responsible for making skin wrinkle but most scientists now think this is not the case. Almost all wrinkling of the face and hands is due to sunlight. Sunbathing, especially for fair-skinned people, is very damaging. It also causes skin cancer. The number of cases of this disease (called malignant melanoma) has been rising over the last 50 years.

To fight the effect of free radicals, the Russian doctors now make their astronauts take lots of vitamins and do lots of exercise. There may be clues here about how to fight the effects of aging. Human beings now eat mostly cooked food. Many vitamins are destroyed by cooking. Perhaps we need to increase the amounts of raw food in our diet to give us more vitamins.

Feeling secure. This little Chinese boy is more likely to grow strong and healthy than a child who is unloved.

Keeping fit. Exercise can help to keep you young.

Active aging

Exercise becomes even more important for health as we get older. In Canada, groups of 60- and 70-year olds were encouraged to follow quite energetic exercises. After a month or so, they were tested and shown to have become "younger" in blood pressure, heart rate, and ability to do mental tasks. It is clear that the third stage need not be one of gradual decline of physical and mental states. It can be very active and should be enjoyable.

A generation gap? Young people and old can help each other in many ways. Everyone needs to feel useful in one way or another.

A gift of extra time

Three hundred years ago, the British thinker Thomas Hobbes described human life as "poor, nasty, brutish and short." For many of the world's poor this may still be true. But for many in rich countries it is no longer true. For most people, at least one quarter of their lives will be spent not at school, or work, or bringing up a family. This is a whole new era in human development. In the twenty-first century one of the great choices for all of us will be how to use this valuable extra time.

The health of older people depends on the same kinds of needs that the young have. Older people need to feel they are worthwhile and needed, just as young people do. Building new ways for people to contribute their talents, ideas, skills, and experience as they get older will do more for health care than any amount of new drugs, operations, or wonderful medical technology. We will all be old one day. Let us get the best foundations for a long, healthy, happy life now. Health is a choice we should all make, the sooner, the better.

Fit for Thought?
- How do you spend your leisure time? (Thinking about sports, watching television, etc.) Find out how older people in your family spend their leisure time. How do you think people in the future will use the time when they are not working? Think about people in developing countries, too.

Glossary

antibiotic – a drug that slows down the growth and reproduction of bacteria. The body's own immune system then deals with the infection.

antibodies – chemicals produced by some white blood cells to fight diseases. Antibodies combine with antigens to make them harmless. Other white blood cells then destroy the antigens.

antigens – any chemical that causes antibodies to be produced. Antigens cause illness if they are not contained by antibodies.

bacteria – a group of simple, single-celled organisms growing in all environments. Some can cause disease. Most are helpful and essential to the ecology of the planet.

cancer – an abnormal growth of cells. Eventually they can break from the original site in the body and move into other organs.

chromosomes – long strings of DNA found in the nucleus of all cells. They can be thought of as strings of genes. Humans have pairs of chromosomes, receiving one of each pair from the mother and the other one from the father.

ecology – the study of how all living things interact with their environment.

environment – the surroundings in which plants and animals live and which provide them with what they need to live.

epidemic – an outbreak of disease affecting a large number of people.

fungus – a plant-like organism without green color that feeds on dead or living plant or animal matter. Some fungi can cause infections if they get into the skin (ringworm, athlete's foot) or mouth (some gum infections).

gene – a code for a trait that passes from parents to offspring. Each gene is in the form of a chemical code. Genes are linked together, making up the bulk of chromosomes.

HIV – two kinds of virus that destroy the white blood cells of the immune system. It is spread mainly by unprotected sexual contact, contaminated hypodermic needles, and infected blood. The worst affected part of the world is Uganda, where there are now tens of thousands of orphans whose parents have died with the fatal form of the disease, AIDS.

organs – single units of the body, such as the heart, lungs, kidneys, brain.

organisms – living things, such as plants and animals. (**Microscopic organisms** are so small they can only be seen through a microscope.)

tissues – the materials of the body made up of many cells. In a single tissue, such as muscle, nerve, or liver, all the cells have the same job.

vaccination – prevention from disease by giving antigens made from disease-causing organisms, such as bateria and viruses.

virus – a microscopic form that has some traits of living things—can only reproduce inside living material. A virus has little more structure than a protein coating around a package of chemicals containing its genes. Viruses cause many diseases, such as the common cold, chicken pox, and AIDS.

Further Reading

Aaseng, Nathan *The Disease Fighters: The Nobel Prize in Medicine* (Lerner Pubns. Co. 1987)

AIDS: What Does It Mean to You? (Walker & Co. 1987)

Asimov, Isaac *How Did We Find Out About Blood?* (Walker & Co. 1986)

Flint, S. Jane *Viruses* (Carolina Biological Supply 1988)

Gutnik, Martin *Genetics* (Watts 1985)

Hampton, J. *World Health* (Rourke Corp.)

Health Care Delivery Dale C. Garett & Solomon H. Snyder, editors (Chelsea House 1989)

Lo Pinto, Richard *Pollution* (Carolina Biological Supply 1988)

Ward, Brian R. *Diet and Nutrition* (Watts 1987)

——— *Health and Hygiene* (Watts 1988)

Index

acupuncture 40
AIDS (HIV) 12, 14, 17
alcohol 16
alternative medicine 40
anesthetics 20
anthrax 18
antibodies 12, 13, 14, 17
antigens 14, 17
aromatherapy 40
artificial joints 26
asthma 33, 35
Australia 8

bacteria 14, 17
barefoot doctors 26
bees 23
brain (mind) 38, 39, 40, 41

California 6
cancer 20, 22, 36, 37, 39, 42
catheters 28
Central African Republic 7
cerebral palsy 26–28
China 20, 22, 26, 37
cholera 7, 8
colds 12
Colombia 16
computer-aided design 26–28
corals 10
curare 20
cystic fibrosis 12

dengue fever 17
Denmark 8
diabetes 19, 20
diarrhea 7, 23
diet 36, 37, 38
drugs 18, 19, 20, 21, 22, 38

ecology 35
endoscopes 25, 28

England (Britain) 6, 7, 8, 16, 17, 19, 20, 22, 28, 33, 36, 37, 39
exercise 40, 41, 43

farming 32, 34, 35
flu (influenza) 12, 22
France 7

genes 11, 12, 13
genetic engineering 12, 13
genome 12, 13
Germany 18, 28
Ghana 17

hay fever 23
heart attacks 36, 37
heart surgery 28
Holland 8

immune system 14, 17
India 7, 38
industry 30, 31, 32
infant mortality 7, 9
Italy 17

Japan 8, 25

"keyhole surgery" 28
Korea 20

lasers 24, 25, 29
lead 32
leukemia 20, 22
lieshmaniasis 17

malaria 17
measles 7, 8
microbes 10

New Zealand 8
Norway 8

osteoporosis 28

parasites 23
placebo 38
pollution 7, 8, 9, 32, 33, 34
psoriasis 20

rain forests 20
reflexology 40
renin 22

scanners 25–26, 28
scarlet fever 8
Spain 17
Sweden 8
symptoms 26, 28, 29
synthetic drugs 18, 23

Tanzania 26
tobacco 16
tomography 25, 29
Computer-Aided Tomography (CAT) 25
tuberculosis 7

ulcers 24
United Nations 4, 8
United States 7, 8, 12, 16, 17, 19, 22, 25, 26, 28, 32, 34, 36
U.S.S.R. (Russia) 30, 42

vaccines 14, 16, 22
viruses 12, 14, 15, 17
vitamins 38, 42

white blood cells 14, 15
whooping cough 8

yoga 40

First published in England, 1990,
by Evans Brothers Ltd., London

12257

DATE DUE			Metro Litho Oak Forest, IL 60452
MAR 19 1992			
APR 22 1992			
MAY 13 1992			
192			
JUN 03 1992			
OCT 19 94			
APR 07 98			

2801-X

613   Collinson, Alan
COL -   Choosing health